Blue Lake

Carmel Reilly

Contents

Blue Lake

Blue Lake is in a park,
not far from the middle of the city.

Lots of people visit Blue Lake every day.
Many of them come to sit near the water,
or go walking or running around the lake.
Others go sailing, fishing or bird watching.

Blue Lake is a beautiful place
where there are always lots of things happening.

Blue Lake is not very wide, but it is quite long.
It has an island in the middle that is covered with tall grass.

Lots of trees grow on the banks of the lake.
There is a track along the side of the lake
for walking and running.

At one end of the lake, there is a **jetty** where boats can be tied up.
Near the jetty is a café, where people often stop to buy something to eat.

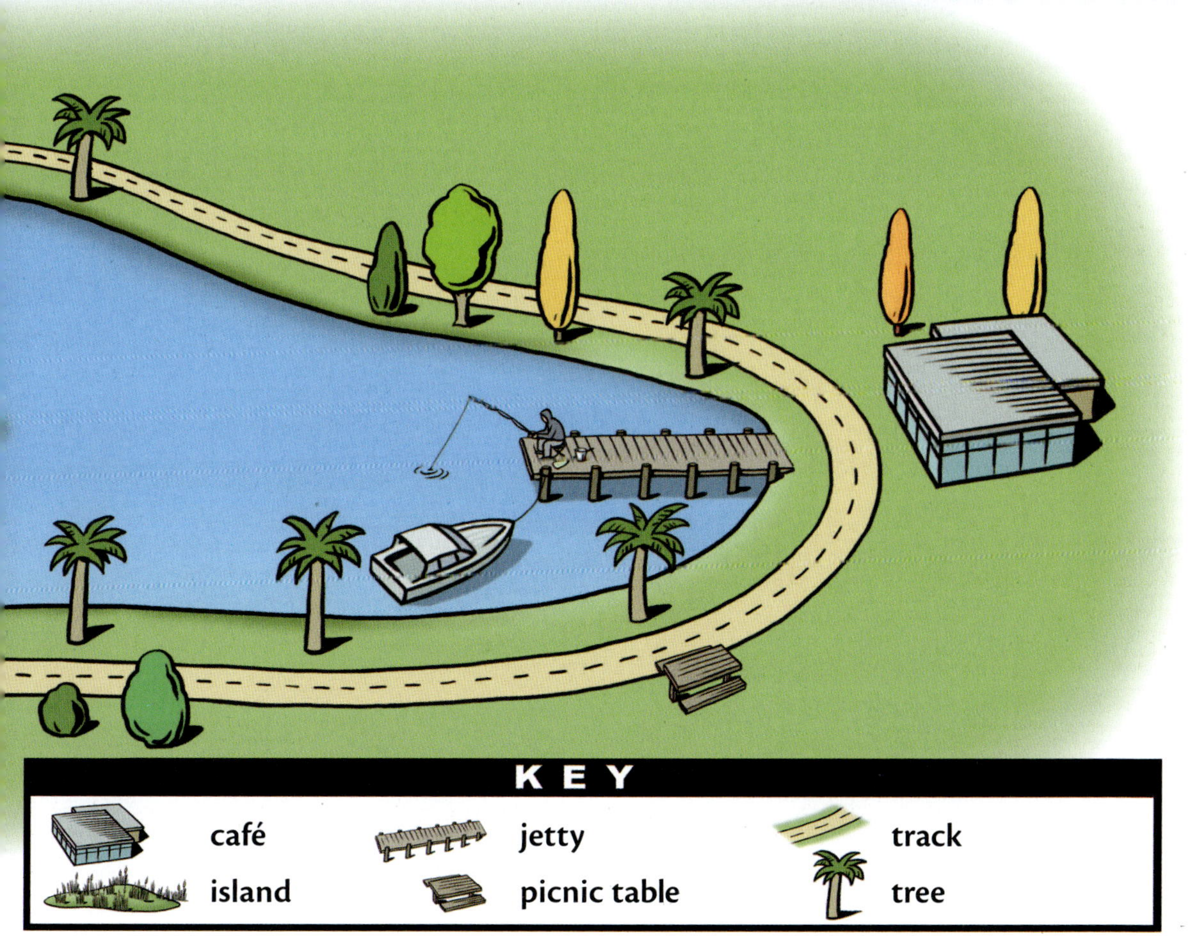

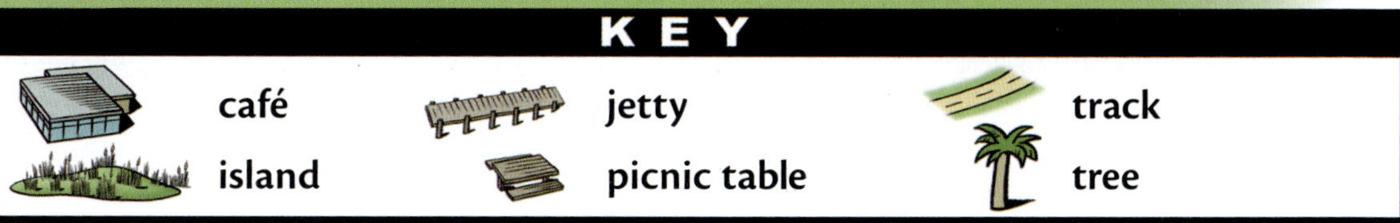

Plants and Animals

Many kinds of plants grow in the water and along the banks of the lake.

Fish and **eels** swim in the water, and more than 100 kinds of birds live close by. Many of these birds live by eating the fish and water plants.

Some birds build their nests in the grass or in trees on the banks of the lake.

Other animals, such as small rats, bats and reptiles, live around the lake, too.

Visitors to Blue Lake

A lot of people come to the lake every day.
Some of them like to sit on the banks and look at the water.
Many have picnics on the grass or at the tables close by.

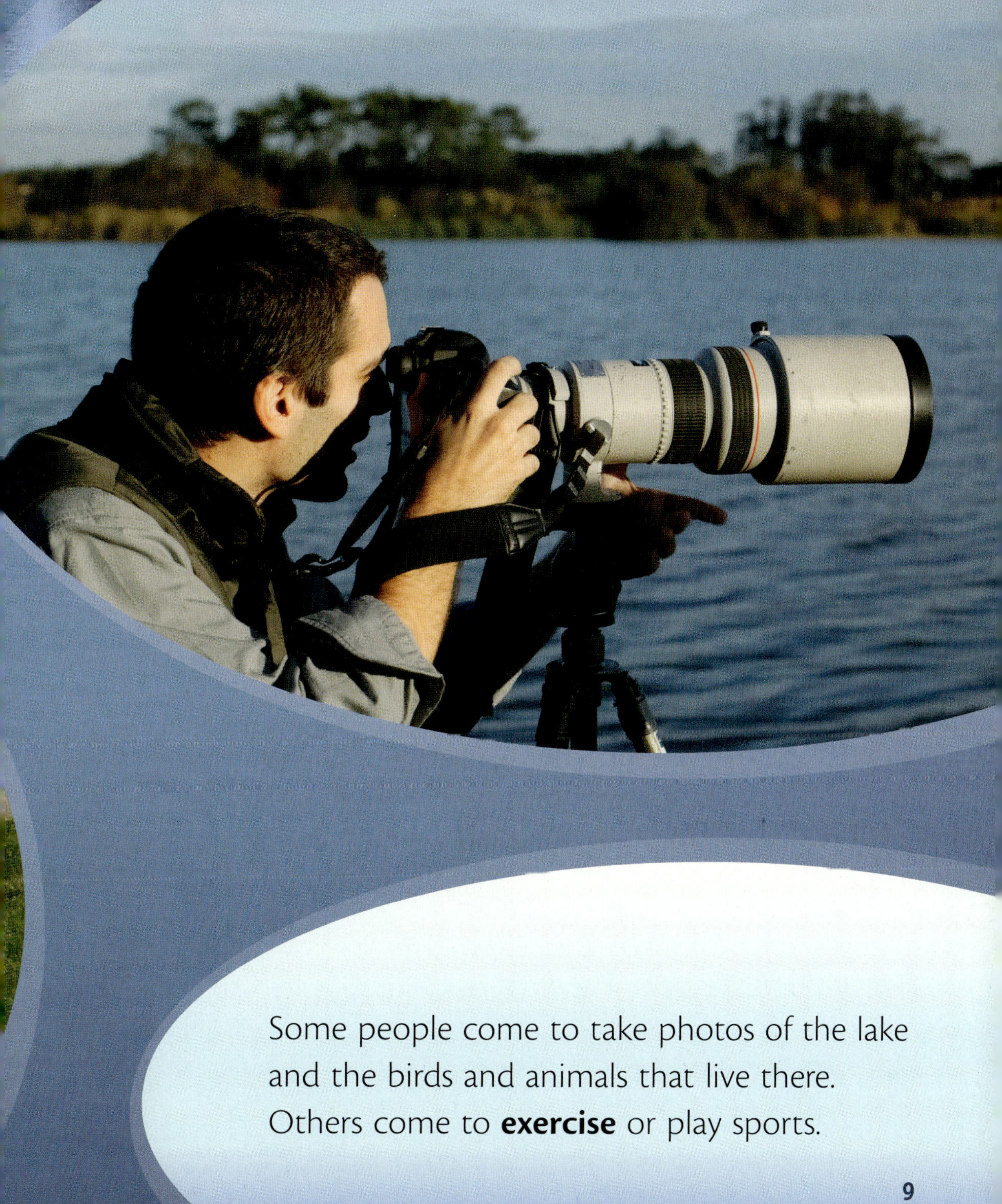

Some people come to take photos of the lake and the birds and animals that live there. Others come to **exercise** or play sports.

Sailing, Rowing and Fishing

Lots of people come to the lake to go sailing. Some people like to sail for fun. Others like to take part in the races that are held there every weekend.

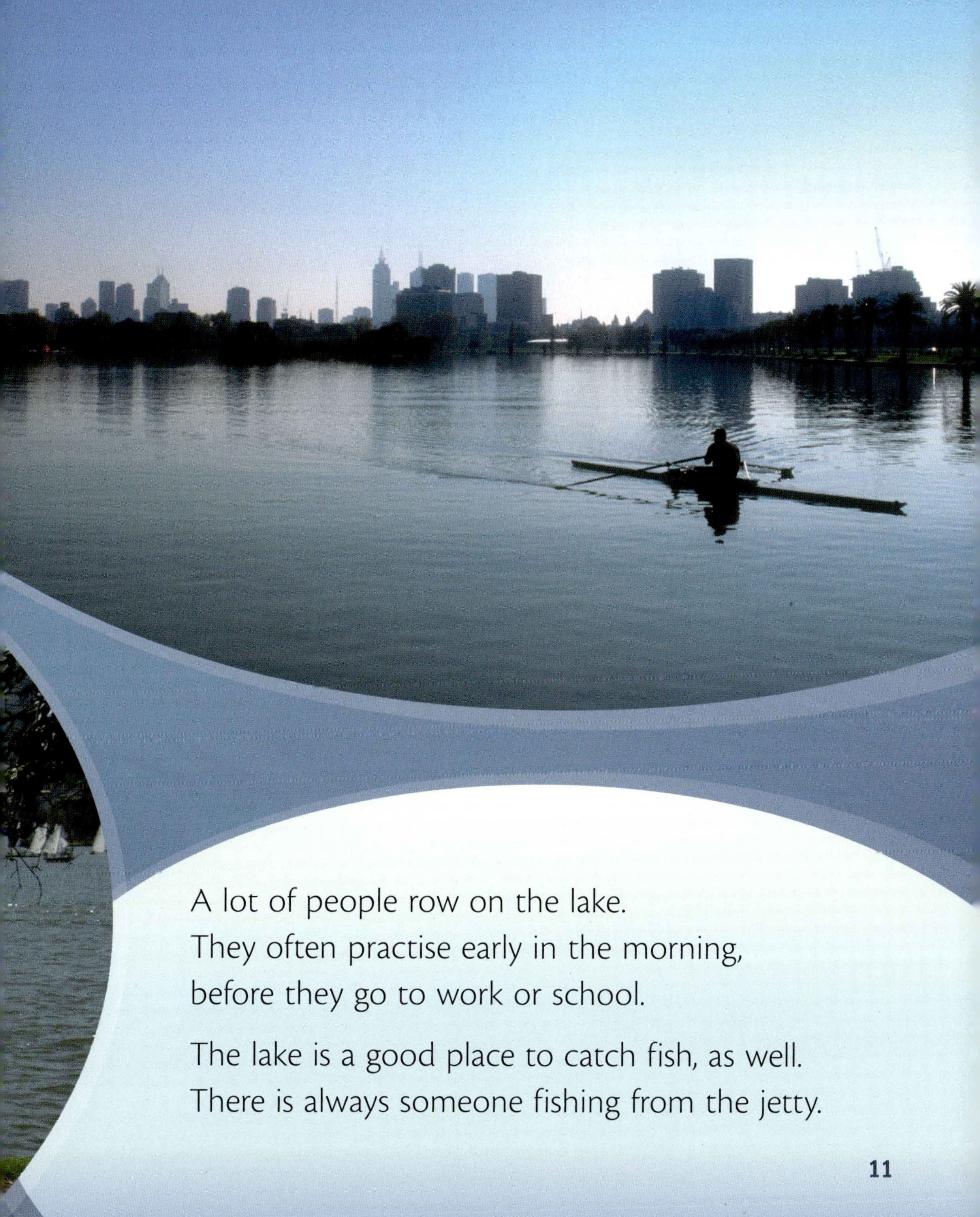

A lot of people row on the lake.
They often practise early in the morning,
before they go to work or school.

The lake is a good place to catch fish, as well.
There is always someone fishing from the jetty.

Park Rangers

A team of **park rangers** looks after the lake.
The rangers check that the plants and animals in and around the lake are healthy.
They check that the water is clean, and take away any rubbish that has been left behind.

The rangers ask people not to feed the birds at the lake.
Birds need to find their own food, like plants and fish.
Bread can make birds sick.

A Great Place for Everyone

Blue Lake is a great place to visit. People who like sport can go walking, running, sailing or fishing.

People who want some quiet time
can rest on the banks and watch the birds.
There is something for everyone to do at Blue Lake.

Glossary

eels (*noun*)	fish with long bodies that look like snakes
exercise (*verb*)	to be active to stay fit and healthy
jetty (*noun*)	a place over water where boats can be tied up
park rangers (*noun*)	people who look after parks